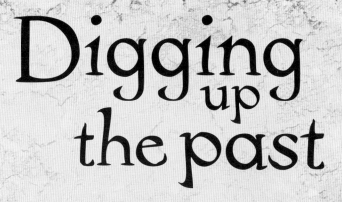

Digging
up
the past

Lisa Jane Gillespie

Designed by Sam Chandler
and Josephine Thompson

Illustrated by Maria Cristina Pritelli

Archaeology consultant: Dr. Tony Pollard, University of Glasgow
Reading consultant: Alison Kelly, Senior Lecturer, Roehampton University

Contents

3 Hidden history

4 Signs and clues

6 Dig in

8 Palaces and huts

10 Ancient people

12 A buried town

14 Art from long ago

16 Underwater past

18 Ancient tombs

20 War stories

22 Standing tall

24 What's the date?

26 Model buildings

28 Preserving the past

30 Glossary

31 Websites to visit

32 Index

People who dig things up to learn about the past are called archaeologists (say *ark-ee-ol-o-jists*). You'll find out more about them in this book.

Hidden history

Things from long ago sometimes get buried underground. Slowly, layers of soil build up over them and plants or buildings cover them.

Ancient things, like these jewels, help experts to understand how people lived in the past.

Signs and clues

Archaeologists look for different clues that tell them where something might be buried.

Lumps and bumps on the ground can mark where old buildings once stood. These grassy bumps show where an old fortress used to be.

Old coins or pieces of tile can be washed up by rivers. This may mean more are buried nearby.

Ancient pots are sometimes found in fields. Experts search the area to try to find more.

Everyday objects such as tools can be found buried near ruins and old buildings.

Sometimes machines such as metal detectors are used to help to find things underground.

Beep!

Dig in

Archaeologists only begin to dig when they think they know where something is buried.

1. Often, they use shovels to remove the top layer of soil.

2. They use trowels to search through the soil very carefully.

3. If they find something fragile, they brush it clean.

4. Then they take it away to preserve and study it.

This archaeologist has dug up the bones of someone who died long ago. She is cleaning them with a soft brush.

Palaces and huts

Buried buildings can give many clues about what life was like in the past.

This ancient palace was dug up in Greece. It belonged to a rich king and had hundreds of rooms with beautiful paintings on the walls.

Thousands of years ago, people in Europe lived in simple round huts. The remains of some of them have been dug up.

The remains helped experts to find out how ancient people built the huts. First, they dug lots of holes and stood wooden posts in them.

Then, they made a wall from sticks and mud. They used poles to make a frame for the roof. They covered this with straw.

Ancient people

Sometimes the remains of ancient people and clothes are dug up. Experts study them to find out how people looked long ago.

In 1991, a man's body was found frozen in ice on a mountain in Italy.

Scientists did lots of tests on the body. They discovered it was 5,000 years old.

This is what the man might have looked like, when he was alive.

Archaeologists can find out what a person's face looked like, just by studying a skull.

These leather shoes were found in mud near a river. They are 600 years old.

Old shoes and clothes show what people liked to wear in the past.

A buried town

The ancient Roman town of Pompeii in Italy was buried in ash 2,000 years ago when a volcano exploded. Thousands of people died.

All the ruins in this photograph were dug up. They have helped experts to find out what the town was like.

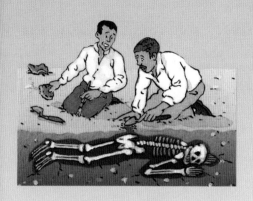

There were holes
in the hardened
ash where bodies
had rotted away.

Archaeologists
carefully poured
plaster into the holes
left by the bodies.

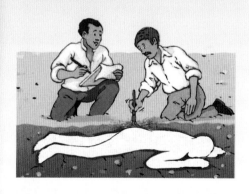

When the plaster
set hard, they broke
away the ash and dug
up the plaster shape.

Some unbroken eggs were even
found preserved in the ash.

Art from long ago

Sometimes archaeologists dig up ancient jewels, carvings and paintings. In 2009, these gold and silver ornaments were found in a field in England.

Experts think someone buried them around a thousand years ago, to keep them safe.

This 500 year old mask is from Mexico. It's made from shells and turquoise stones and shows the face of a god.

In Australia there are some rock paintings of kangaroos that are 20,000 years old.

Underwater past

Things from the past are sometimes found at the bottom of rivers, lakes or oceans.

These divers are studying pots from a shipwreck off the coast of Turkey. The pots contained wine.

1. A ship called the Mary Rose sank in 1545. Divers found it 340 years later.

2. Experts carefully tied the remains of the ship to a huge metal frame.

3. They attached cables to the frame and lifted the ship out of the water.

4. The divers found lots of cannons and weapons beside the shipwreck, too.

Sometimes mini submarines are used to explore shipwrecks.

Ancient tombs

In the past, many dead people were buried in tombs. Sometimes, amazing things were buried with them.

These statues are known as the Terracotta Army. They were discovered in the tomb of a Chinese emperor who died 2,000 years ago.

In 1922, a tomb was discovered buried under sand in the desert in Egypt.

The tomb was full of statues and treasure. It belonged to a king called Tutankhamun.

This golden coffin was found deep in the tomb. It is decorated to show Tutankhamun's face and jewels.

War stories

Some archaeologists try to find out about wars that were fought in the past. They dig on battlefields and look for old weapons.

Divers found this plane in the Pacific Ocean. It crashed during an air battle in World War II.

A team of experts dug at Little Bighorn, USA, where a famous battle was fought in 1876.

They found bullets, arrowheads and bones, and marked where each thing was found.

This helped them to find out what happened during the battle.

Standing tall

Some amazing buildings and statues from the past were never buried.

These giant stone statues stand on Easter Island in the Pacific Ocean. People carved them using simple stone tools around a thousand years ago.

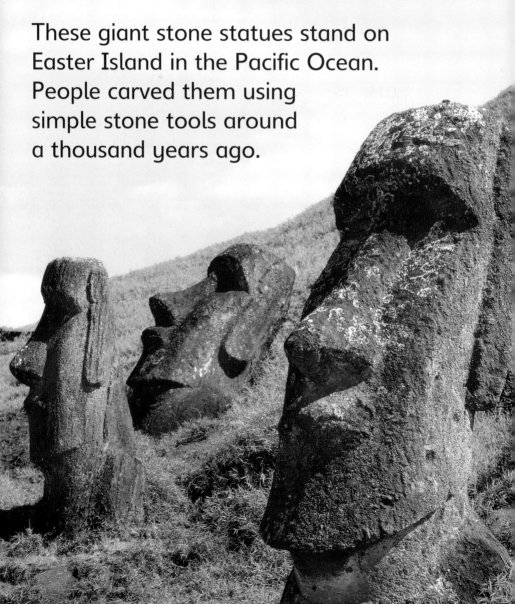

1. The pyramids in Egypt are huge tombs where ancient kings were buried.

2. Each pyramid was made from thousands of huge stone blocks.

3. Teams of workers pulled the blocks into position using wooden sleds.

4. As a pyramid grew, the workers dragged the blocks up ramps made from sand.

Long ago, no one knew how huge stones were moved in ancient times. Some people thought giants lifted them.

What's the date?

Archaeologists have lots of ways of finding out the age of the things they dig up.

Some things, such as coins, have the year they were made stamped on them.

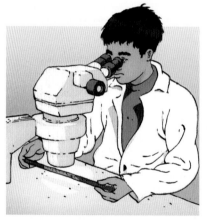

Scientific tests can tell the age of things made from some natural materials, such as wood.

If the age of one object is known, it's likely that other things of the same style are the same age.

Sometimes lots of things are buried in the same place. Usually, the deeper the things are buried, the older they are.

Ground level, today

Coins, 240 years old

Floor tiles, 700 years old

Remains of a wall, 900 years old

Jug, 1,800 years old

Iron sword, 2,200 years old

Model buildings

Sometimes experts use computers to make models of ancient buildings. This helps archaeologists to find out more about them.

1. The remains of the buildings are measured and photographed.

2. All the photos and measurements are carefully entered into a computer.

This is a computer model of an ancient palace. It was part of a huge city in Iran, called Persepolis.

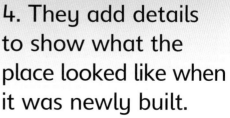

3. Then experts use a program to turn the information into a model on screen.

4. They add details to show what the place looked like when it was newly built.

Preserving the past

Things that have been buried for hundreds of years are often fragile or broken. Experts take care of them, to stop them from falling apart.

Archaeologists in England found pieces of wood with Roman writing on them.

Experts cleaned the pieces carefully and stuck some of them back together.

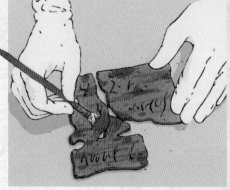

The wood was a party invitation, sent by a Roman lady to her friend.

This ancient metal helmet was rebuilt from hundreds of tiny pieces. It is now on display in a museum for visitors to see.

Some ancient statues can never be put back together. Their noses, heads or arms have never been found.

Glossary

Here are some of the words in this book you might not know. This page tells you what they mean.

 archaeologist – a person who learns about the past by digging things up.

 ruins – old or abandoned buildings, or parts of buildings.

 metal detector – a machine that beeps if it finds something metal.

 trowel - a pointed tool archaeologists use for digging.

 preserve - to protect something so it doesn't rot away.

 remains – what's left of old bodies or ancient objects.

 tomb – a place where an important person is buried.

Websites to visit

You can visit exciting websites to find out more about digging up history.

To visit these websites, go to the Usborne Quicklinks Website at **www.usborne-quicklinks.com** Read the internet safety guidelines, and then type the keywords "**beginners digging**".

The websites are regularly reviewed and the links in Usborne Quicklinks are updated. However, Usborne Publishing is not responsible, and does not accept liability, for the content or availability of any website other than its own. We recommend that children are supervised while on the internet.

These clay statues were dug up in Nigeria. They were made around 2,000 years ago.

Index

archaeologist, 2, 6-7, 13, 20-21, 24, 26, 28, 30
battle, 20-21
bodies, 10, 13
bones, 7, 21
buildings, 5, 8-9, 12, 26-27
clothes, 10-11
coins, 5, 24-25
gold, 3, 14, 19
helmet, 29
huts, 9
jewels, 3, 14, 19

palace, 8, 26-27
plane, 20
pots, 16
preserving, 28-29, 30
pyramids, 23
mask, 15
metal detector, 5, 30
ornaments, 3, 14
ruins, 5, 8, 12, 30
shipwreck, 16-17
statues, 18, 22, 29, 31
tomb, 18-19, 23, 30
town, 12
trowel, 6, 30

Acknowledgements

Photographic manipulation by Nick Wakeford and John Russell
Photo research by Ruth King

Photo credits
The publishers are grateful to the following for permission to reproduce material:
© Daniel Aguilar/Reuters/CORBIS 7; © akg-images /CDA/Guillemot 31; © BAA, Oxford Archaeology and Wessex Archaeology 1; © Jonathan Blair/CORBIS 16; © CG Textures backgrounds 6-7, 18-19, 20-21, 28-29, 30-31; © De Agostini/Getty Images 12; © Ingo Jezierski/Photolibrary.com cover photograph; © Tony Kurdzuk/Star Ledger/CORBIS 19; © Persepolis3d.com 26-27; © Morales Morales/Photolibrary.com 18; © Museum of London 11; © REUTERS/Eddie Keogh 14; © Stella Stella/Photolibrary.com 8; © Superstock/Photolibrary.com 22; © The Trustees of the British Museum 3, 15, 29; © Adrian Warren/www.lastrefuge.co.uk 4; © Mirko Zanni/Photolibrary.com 20

 Sun, moon and stars

 Farm animals

 Elizabeth I

 RUBBISH AND RECYCLING

 Dogs

 Horses and ponies

 Spiders

 Planes

 Ancient Greeks

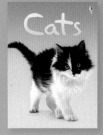 Cats

 VOLCANOES

 DINOSAURS

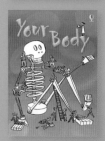 Your Body

 Armour

 Sharks

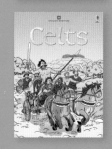 Celts

 Vikings

 Castles

 How flowers grow

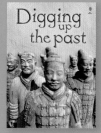 Digging up the past

Living in space

Caterpillars and Butterflies

Ballet

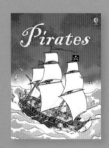
Pirates

Egyptians

Eggs and Chicks

Romans

Weather

Tadpoles and frogs

Why do we eat?

Under the sea

Bears

Aztecs

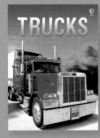
TRUCKS

Night Animals

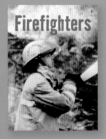
Firefighters

Antarctica

Bugs

COWBOYS

Planet Earth